Greatest
MOMENTS OF
SNOOKER

This edition first published in the UK in 2007
By Green Umbrella Publishing

© Green Umbrella Publishing 2008

www.gupublishing.co.uk

Publishers: Jules Gammond and Vanessa Gardner

Printed and bound in China

ISBN: 978-1-906229-42-9

Greatest
MOMENTS OF
SNOOKER

by IAN WELCH

CONTENTS

CONTENTS

LEGENDARY JOE DAVIS BEATS BROTHER FRED
1940

When Joe Davis won the 1940 world championship he stretched his unbeaten run to 14 successive years. That year's tournament also made history by needing the first ever deciding frame in the history of the event. Joe enjoyed a period of domination in the sport that has been unrivalled since, although his brother Fred did dominate the 1950s to a lesser degree.

Joe Davis was born on 15 April 1901 in Whitwell, a mining village in Derbyshire, and he began to show his talent with a cue after his parents took over the Queen's Hotel when he was 10. The youngster was allowed to practice on the pub's billiard table and four years later Joe went to work at a billiards hall. There he preyed on unsuspecting customers and won enough money to turn professional in 1919.

While he was runner-up in the World Billiards Championship in 1926 – he would eventually win 10 titles – he had to wait until the following year for the inaugural World Snooker Championship. The tournament had been Joe's idea and he organised the event with matches taking place at Thurston's Hall and the final being contested at Birmingham's Camkin's Hall.

There were 10 entrants to the tournament that saw four men compete in a first round to win the opportunity of a place in the quarter-finals. While the first two rounds saw the two competitors play the best of 15 frames, Joe's quarter-final saw all frames played, with Davis winning 10-5. The same would happen in Joe's matches in the semi-final (16-7 in the best of 23) and the final (20-11 in the best of 31). The trophy that would be awarded to the winner cost £19 and was paid for from the players' entry fees. As luck would have it Joe won the tournament and the £6 10s prize money.

Joe went on to win the next 12 championships in succession but in 1940 it became a family affair when he met brother Fred in the final. The match went right down to the wire but the elder Davis eventually triumphed by 37 frames to 36. It was the closest ever final, the narrowest winning margin in previous years having been in 1934 when Joe exacted revenge over Tom Newman – his conqueror in the 1926 World Billiards Championship – with a score of 25-23.

LEGENDARY JOE DAVIS BEATS BROTHER FRED

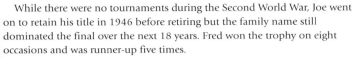

While there were no tournaments during the Second World War, Joe went on to retain his title in 1946 before retiring but the family name still dominated the final over the next 18 years. Fred won the trophy on eight occasions and was runner-up five times.

Fred Davis was born on 13 August 1913 in Whittingham Moor, Chesterfield, and mirrored his elder brother's skill on a billiards table, turning professional in 1929. He joined Joe as a professional snooker player eight years later with their 1940 clash being the only time the two brothers met in the final. Fred decided to call it a day in 1957 but came out of retirement seven years later and became a mainstay of the television series *Pot Black* in the 1970s. He was awarded the MBE in 1977 and the following year reached the semi-finals of the World Championship in Sheffield.

He went on to claim the World Billiards Championship in 1980 and 1981 before making his last appearance at the Crucible in 1984. He eventually retired at the age of 78 in 1992 and died on 16 April 1998.

It was common for billiards champions of the late 19th and early 20th centuries to have cues named after them by manufacturers, and snooker champions followed suit in the mid 20th century. Joe Davis was no exception and a variety of cues were produced that honoured his highest breaks. Please bear in mind that Sydney Smith had registered the first clearance of the table in 1936 with a score of 133. Horace Lindrum held the record for the highest break from the late 1930s until the mid 1940s with 141 until Walter Donaldson made a 142 in 1946. Joe Davis didn't record his first maximum 147 until 1955 and by that time he had retired from competing in the World Championship. This break came in an exhibition match at Leicester Square.

Joe – a keen supporter of Derby County Football Club who even visited the changing room at Wembley to give his own message of support to the players before their 1946 FA Cup triumph over Charlton Athletic – became the sport's first celebrity and was awarded the OBE in 1963. He was even honoured with a waxwork model in Madam Tussauds and his car proudly bore the registration number "CUE 1". Joe Davis died on 10 July 1978, just a few months after watching his younger brother reach that year's semi-finals.

RAY REARDON WINS HIS FOURTH WORLD TITLE
1976

The history of the world championship has seen several players dominate the tournament – Joe Davis in the 1920s and 1930s, Fred Davis in the 1950s and John Pulman in the 1960s – and the 1970s belonged to Ray Reardon. He won the title on six occasions, the first in 1970.

Ray Reardon was born on 8 October 1932 in the Welsh village of Tredegar and his first job on leaving school at the age of 14 was in the local coal mines. Already a keen snooker player, Reardon allegedly wore gloves to protect his hands while working. After being involved in an accident in which he was buried alive in a mineshaft for three hours, Reardon decided that the family trade was not his preferred option and joined the police force.

His amateur career began to take off when he won the *News of the World* title in 1949 and he was also the reigning Welsh amateur champion from 1950 to 1955 when he moved to Stoke. His profile increased when he won the English amateur title in 1964 and took the gamble to turn professional three years later when sponsors persuaded him to leave his job.

Reardon would not have to wait long for success, winning the world title in 1970 with a 37-33 victory over John Pulman. He had entered the 1969 tournament which was the first one since 1951 to be held in a knockout format but found himself losing by the odd frame in 49 to the legendary Fred Davis in their first-round encounter. Reardon recaptured the crown in 1973 and went on to register four consecutive victories. In the first final, he emerged the 38-32 victor over Australian Eddie Charlton in a final that saw some frames shown on the BBC, the first time that the tournament had enjoyed television coverage.

The following year saw him overcome Graham Miles by 22-12 to claim the £2,000 prize money while the 1975 final saw a rematch with Charlton but the Welshman again triumphed, this time by 31 frames to 30 in Nunawading Basketball Centre, Melbourne. It would prove to be the last time the championship was held outside the UK as the following year saw Manchester stage the event before it moved to its permanent home in Sheffield's Crucible Theatre in 1977.

GREATEST MOMENTS OF SNOOKER

The 1976 world championship was the first tournament to be sponsored by Embassy, a partnership that would last 30 years until the ban on tobacco advertising. In the first round, Reardon was paired with John Dunning but saw off this challenge with a frame score of 15-7 before taking on the up-and-coming Dennis Taylor in the quarter-final. With the clash being decided on the best of 29 frames, Reardon soon notched up a 15-2 victory over the previous year's semi-finalist.

His opponent in the semi-final was South African Perrie Mans – a player whom Reardon would triumph over when he won the tournament in 1978 – and he was dispatched by a 20-10 scoreline to set up a meeting with Alex Higgins in the showpiece final. Higgins was the youngest ever winner of the trophy at 23 years of age with his 37-32 victory over John Spencer in 1972 but experience prevailed and Reardon clinched the trophy with a score of 27-16.

Reardon claimed the title and the winner's cheque of £6,000 (Spencer registered the highest break with 138) and wrote his name in the record books as only the fourth man to win four consecutive titles. He would only make one other appearance in the final, again against Higgins in 1982 with the Hurricane gaining his revenge with an 18-15 triumph.

Reardon remained the number one ranked player in the world until 1980-81 but he did recapture that honour after his victory in the 1982 Professional Players Tournament. That victory also gave him the distinction of being the oldest player to ever win a ranking tournament, a record that he still holds to this day.

With the arrival on the circuit of the seemingly invincible Steve Davis – who dominated the scene in the 1980s with eight final appearances that brought him six world titles, Reardon's star faded as his eyesight began to deteriorate with age (although he did reach the semi-finals in 1985) and he retired in 1992. He did not escape the lure of the baize completely, though, and went on to give some help and advice to Ronnie O'Sullivan, one of the superstars of the early 21st century.

Ray Reardon has always been a popular guest on chat shows and regularly appeared on the television quiz show *Big Break*. He has long been an active member of the World Professional Billiards and Snooker Association and still participates in senior's events although you are more likely to find him these days on a golf course near his south Devon home.

TERRY GRIFFITHS, FIRST QUALIFIER TO WIN WORLD TITLE 1979

It's not often that the fairytale comes true for sportsmen but it did for Terry Griffiths in 1979 when he became the first ever qualifier to win the world championship. The fact that he achieved this in only his second professional tournament makes the feat even more remarkable.

Terry Griffiths was born in Llanelli on 16 October 1947 and became a postman after leaving school. He showed his talent on the baize early and claimed the Llanelli and District championship when he was only 16 years of age. He became well known around the amateur circuit in Wales by winning the championship in 1975. He added the English amateur title in 1977 and 1978 before turning professional at the ripe old age of 31 and attaining nationwide popularity the following year.

Griffiths had entered the UK championships in late 1978 but found his professional debut cut short with an 8-9 reverse against Rex Williams in the qualifying round. The following April saw him enter his second professional tournament and the result could not have been more different.

Griffiths – renowned for his slow, methodical style of play – was paired with Perrie Mans in the first round of the 1979 world championships. The South African had finished runner-up to Ray Reardon the previous year but was unable to make it past his first match in 1979, losing 13-8 to the relatively unknown Griffiths. The Welshman's next opponent was Alex Higgins. In a thrilling match, the man from the Principality edged out the Irishman by 13 frames to 12. It was quite a feat for Griffiths as Higgins had become the youngest ever winner of the tournament in 1972 and been the losing finalist in 1976 (he would also finish runner-up in 1980).

This set up a semi-final clash with Australian Eddie Charlton, who had recently been consistently ranked number three in the world. Charlton's claim to fame would be that he was the only man ever to play in the final of both the snooker and billiards world championship finals without winning either. He had finished as runner-up in the snooker championship

TERRY GRIFFITHS, FIRST QUALIFIER TO WIN WORLD TITLE

three times (1968, 1973 and 1975) but enjoyed great popularity winning a hat-trick of *Pot Black* titles (1972, 1973 and 1980).

Still, Griffiths took no notice of reputations and emerged victorious from the semi-final by 19 frames to 17. He was shell-shocked after his victory and made the famous comment "I'm in the final now, you know" in a post-match interview with David Vine.

In the final, Griffiths was paired with Dennis Taylor – another player who was appearing in his first world championship title match. The Llanelli Potter triumphed in the best of 47-frame match with a winning score of 24-16 to claim the title at his first attempt and a cheque for £10,000.

Griffiths followed this with an appearance in the final of the 1979 UK championships. As world champion, he no longer had to face the rigmarole of qualifying for the tournament and registered a 9-4 third-round victory over Cliff Wilson. He emerged victorious from a quarter-final clash with Alex Higgins by 9-7 to set up a meeting with Bill Werbeniuk. The Canadian, famous for having to down numerous pints of lager before and during each match to counteract his nerves, didn't prove too much of an obstacle and went down 3-9.

The final saw Griffiths paired with John Virgo but his opponent got stuck in traffic and was late for the start of the match. In a first for a major final, he was penalised two frames for this delayed entrance and – although Griffiths told the match officials that he didn't want to accept the two frames – won the first two frames of the session to lead 4-0.

During the interval, an apologetic Griffiths went to his opponent and offered to split the prize money only to be told "You haven't won it yet!" As it turned out, Virgo won the match by claiming the last frame to register a 9-8 victory… Three years later saw Griffiths again reach the final of the UK championships, only this time he emerged victorious. Having trailed Alex Higgins 13-15 as the final drew to a close, the Welshman had to win the last three frames which he duly did.

Griffiths also appeared in four Masters finals within the space of five years. He beat Alex Higgins 9-5 in 1980 only to lose to the Irishman 6-9 the following year. It would prove his only triumph in this competition, as he was defeated by Steve Davis (5-9) in 1982 and Jimmy White (5-9) two years later.

Terry Griffiths graced the world championship final on one more occasion, losing 11-18 to Steve Davis in 1988, before retiring in 1997 although he has coached the likes of Stephen Hendry and Mark Williams. He opened the Terry Griffiths Matchroom in his hometown in 1987 that has produced some outstanding players including 2000 world championship runner-up Matthew Stevens.

STEVE DAVIS COMPILES FIRST TELEVISED 147 BREAK 1982

The Lada Classic, sponsored by Lada Cars, was hardly one of the major competitions on the professional snooker circuit in the early 1980s (it did become a ranking tournament in 1984 before the sponsorship was taken over by Mercantile Credit the following year). But Steve Davis's meeting with John Spencer would prove to be a game that is watched time and time again by snooker fans worldwide.

Steve Davis was born on 22 August 1957 in Plumstead, London, and began playing snooker at the age of 12. His father had been a keen snooker player and the young Davis followed in his footsteps. He won the national under-19 billiards championship in 1976 before being talent-spotted by Barry Hearn and signed up. Hearn was an entrepreneurial accountant who had made his fortune by buying and selling snooker halls but he ventured into management in 1974. Founding his now famous Matchroom, Hearn went on to manage top stars such as Davis, Terry Griffiths, Dennis Taylor, Willie Thorne, Neal Foulds, Jimmy White, Cliff Thorburn and Ronnie O'Sullivan while in 1987 he also branched out into managing boxers such as Chris Eubank and Nigel Benn.

Under Hearn's protective and nurturing wing, Davis found himself playing against professionals and turned pro himself after winning the 1978 Pontins Open. He entered the 1979 world championships but lost to Dennis Taylor by 13-11 in the first round. The following year's tournament saw him reach the quarter-finals with victories over Patsy Fagan (10-6) and Terry Griffiths (13-10) before losing 9-13 to eventual runner-up Alex Higgins.

But his professional career really took off in the 1980-81 season. Having seen off the challenge of Mike Hallett (9-1), Bill Werbeniuk (9-3), Tony Meo (9-5) and Terry Griffiths (9-0) in the preceding rounds, he exacted his revenge on Higgins in the final. The youngster cruised to a 16-6 victory that marked the beginning of his dominance of the sport. That stranglehold would last until the arrival of Steve Hendry in the 1990s.

Davis went on to claim the 1981 world championship and retain his UK title as well as becoming champion of both the English Professional and Yamaha International before heading to Oldham's Civic Centre on 11 January 1982.

The Lada Classic match had started off fairly unremarkably but was about to make history in the fifth frame. With the two players tied at two frames apiece, Spencer broke but caught the reds a bit too thickly and eight balls were scattered from the pack. When Davis calmly placed one red in the middle pocket no-one could have anticipated that Spencer would not return to the table that frame.

After potting three reds and two blacks, Davis opened up the remaining reds with an angle off his third black but ended up out of position after his next two shots which prompted the commentator to assume that he would play a safety shot. This was not Steve Davis's plan, however, and he doubled a red into the middle pocket to regain position on the black. He ricocheted off the subsequent black into the pack to ensure that each red ball was now potable.

It took Davis only eight minutes to compile his century and he was looking set to win the Lada car that was the prize for a maximum break with just two reds left on the table. The final red was dispatched, leaving himself the perfect angle after sinking the black to bring the cue ball back up the table for the yellow. With all the colours on their respective spots, it seemed another training exercise for the youngster but everyone appreciated the tension he must be feeling.

He potted the yellow, green and brown but didn't quite line himself up for the blue as he would have liked. With a wry shake of the head, he crouched over the table and registered another five points for the blue but the cue ball settled in a straight line with the pink and black after travelling up and down the table. Reaching for the rest, Davis lined up a shot to the corner pocket and, with massive amounts of screw, regained his position on the black.

As the crowd and commentators alike voiced their encouragement, Davis cleared the last ball from the table and raised his hand to his head as if in disbelief. His opponent quickly congratulated him with a smile and Davis put his cue on the table and perched on the edge, shaking his head while the crowd showed their appreciation of the remarkable achievement they had just witnessed.

Davis – who had won the title the previous year when it was sponsored by Wilsons – again reached the final but lost to Terry Griffiths by nine frames to eight. He remained a dominant force in the final over the next 10 years, however, emerging victorious in 1983, 1984, 1987, 1988 and 1992.

STEVE DAVIS COMPILES FIRST TELEVISED 147 BREAK 21

ALEX HIGGINS WINS WORLD TITLE
1982

Snooker was nearing the peak of its popularity in 1982 and that year's world championships will be remembered for many reasons. The BBC put together a montage of coverage set to Scott Joplin's "The Entertainer" that captured the mood of the nation. The tournament also saw some fantastic matches and culminated in champion Alex Higgins tearfully embracing his wife and baby daughter in front of a worldwide television audience of millions.

There was a change in format for this tournament, with the number of participants being increased from 24 to 32. The top eight seeds had to compete in the first round which meant that every entrant would have to play five matches in order to claim the title and the record prize money of £25,000. The favourites going into the event were Steve Davis and Terry Griffiths, two players who were demolishing all opposition and exhibiting some fantastic snooker but the curse of the Crucible struck yet again.

No reigning champion has ever successfully defended their first title at that venue and 1982 was no exception. Steve Davis had won the previous year's tournament with an 18-12 victory over Doug Mountjoy but he found himself on the wrong end of a 1-10 thrashing at the hands of Tony Knowles in the first round. Even Griffiths himself went out at the first stage, losing 6-10 to Willie Thorne.

Alex Higgins saw off the challenge of Jim Meadowcroft in the first round with a 10-5 scoreline before taking on Doug Mountjoy in the next round. The Welshman put up a brave battle but Higgins claimed the narrowest of victories by a 13-12 margin. He then met Willie Thorne in the quarter-final but emerged unscathed from that encounter with a 13-10 triumph to set up a semi-final clash with the relatively unknown Jimmy White.

Ray Reardon started off his competition by disposing of Jim Donnelly in the first round. Although the Scotsman put up a brave fight, he was no match for the veteran Welshman who notched up a 10-5 victory. Reardon's second-round opponent was John Virgo who was

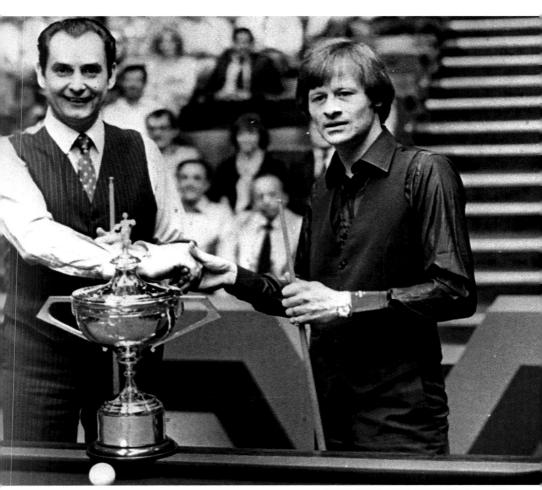

dispatched by a similar winning margin, at 13-8. Silvino Francisco stood in Reardon's way in the quarter-final and the South African had made good progress considering this was his first attempt at this competition. Reardon, however, was in no mood to be charitable and won the match 13-8.

The semi-finals saw a classic encounter between six-time champion Reardon and Eddie Charlton, who had twice finished runner-up. The match ebbed and flowed but neither player could establish a winning margin. That all changed when Reardon put together a hat-trick of frames with the score tied at 11-11. The 26th frame rolled back the years as Reardon put together a classic 98 break to demoralise the Australian, and Dracula – as he was affectionately known because of his prominent widow's peak – clinched his 16th frame to secure a place in the final.

In the other semi-final, Higgins took on 20-year-old Jimmy White who was the only unseeded player to reach the last four. This match has since become regarded as one of the greatest ever witnessed at the Crucible. With the score at 8-6 to White, both players made mistakes in the 15th frame but Higgins managed to claw back the deficit to a single frame. But White kept plugging away at the older man and extended his lead to 11-8 with a break of 89 that came to an end when he missed the last red.

By the time the 29th frame had been played (in a best out of 31 match), White led 15-14 and needed just one more to claim his place in the final. Higgins, however, was not about to give up and got his chance after the young Londoner missed a simple black and had to be content with a break of 41 in the penultimate frame. The Irishman was unfortunate as the cue ball ended safely nestled in against the reds and White added another 18 points before rattling a red in the jaws of the corner pocket. Higgins made no mistake and registered a break of 69 to tie the score at 15 frames apiece. Higgins claimed the final frame with some masterful play to leave White distraught at not having been able to clinch the match when he had been in the better position.

The final proved to be a thrilling spectacle as well, with Higgins claiming his second world crown by an 18-15 scoreline in what proved to be both men's last appearance in the world championship final. Although the Welshman reached the semi-final in 1985 – the same year he thrashed Steve Davis 5-0 in the British Open – he slid down the rankings and retired in 1992. Higgins' career, meanwhile, has since slid downhill amid controversy and a battle with throat cancer.

CLIFF THORBURN, 147 AT WORLD CHAMPIONSHIPS 1983

The second round of the 1983 world championships saw the competition's first ever maximum 147 break when Canadian Cliff Thorburn took on Terry Griffiths. Thorburn had eased past John Campbell 10-5 in the first round while the Welshman had beaten Mark Wildman 10-8.

The fourth frame started out as a cagey affair with both players trying to leave the white safe after the reds had been scattered across the table. Trailing 1-2 Griffiths, however, fouled and Thorburn stepped up to the table. Taking his time, he carefully lined up a red but it rattled in the jaws of the corner pocket before running back along the cushion and knocking another red into the opposite pocket. It is perhaps ironic that such luck would trigger a historic break.

He made no mistake with the subsequent black and quickly ran up a score of 80 from 10 reds and 10 blacks as Griffiths sat, quietly reflecting on his misfortune. Thorburn lost position slightly after the 12th red but potted the black despite the awkward queuing angle. After the 14th red, Thorburn relieved the tension in the theatre by making a quip about having a break and then blowing his nose and wiping his hands before regaining his composure to finish the job in hand.

Fellow Canadian Bill Werbeniuk was playing his second-round match against David Taylor on the other table but paused to watch the excitement. Thorburn made no mistake with the remaining red and headed for the colours. Professional snooker players spend hours potting the colours from their respective spots so it presents less of a problem than clearing all the reds.

His shot to pot the final black, however, left him short of the yellow and it required a longer shot than he would have liked to start clearing the colours. He sank each one with textbook accuracy and dropped to his knees while punching the air when the break was finally over. Griffiths and Werbeniuk joined him in an embrace that signalled just what this achievement meant in front of the millions watching on television.

Thorburn completed his maximum score to claim the £3,000 prize for the highest break, £5,000 for the championship break and £10,000 for a 147. He went on to defeat Griffiths by 13 frames to 12 (finishing at an incredibly late 3.51am) to set up a quarter-final meeting with another Canadian in Kirk Stevens. In another closely-fought match, Thorburn edged out Stevens by 13-12 before again going down to the last frame against Tony Knowles.

Tragically, though, Thorburn's wife miscarried shortly before the match and this affected his mental preparations. He met Steve Davis in the final – a player who was at his best – and lost 18-6, the biggest winning margin in the final at that time. Davis won his second world title and would go on to claim another four before the end of the decade.

Cliff Thorburn was born on 16 January 1948 and had been runner-up in the world championships in 1977 but had conquered Alex Higgins in 1980 to become the only overseas player to ever claim the title. He went on to reach the quarter-finals for the next two years before going one better in 1986. Unfortunately, he was again pitted against Steve Davis with the three-time champion emerging a 16-12 winner. He went out at the first attempt to Dene O'Kane in 1987 before another semi-final meeting with Steve Davis the following year that finished 16-8 to the Englishman.

The last year of the 1980s saw Thorburn fined £10,000 for using cocaine and suspended for two matches but he returned to the Crucible in 1990 to battle through to the quarter-final where he lost 13-6 to John Parrott. It would be another four years before Thorburn again graced the world championships but he exited at the first-round stage with a 10-9 defeat by Nigel Bond. That would prove to be his last appearance at the Crucible before retiring in 1996, although he did return 10 years later to unveil a life-size painting of his famous break. Painted by Michael Myers – not to be confused with the Canadian comedy actor of the same name – the picture is now on display at the Macdonald St Paul's Hotel in Sheffield.

Although now professionally retired, Cliff Thorburn – who was awarded the Order of Canada in 1984 – does still play snooker and occasionally enters competitions in his native Canada. He has also opened a snooker club in Toronto and regularly renews his acquaintance with countrymen Kirk Stevens and Jim Wych. There has been a lack of quality Canadian snooker players competing in England in recent years with the reason being suggested that they prefer the North American pool circuit where there are far greater financial rewards.

DENNIS TAYLOR BEATS STEVE DAVIS 18-17
1985

The 1985 world championship final between Steve Davis and Dennis Taylor set many records and has been hailed as the greatest game of snooker ever seen. More than 18 million people tuned in their televisions to watch an encounter that at 14 hours and 50 minutes broke the record for the longest 35-frame match. The viewing figures remain a record for BBC2 and signified the largest British audience for any sporting event at that time and the largest after-midnight television audience.

Reigning champion Davis was the favourite going into the final and took the first eight frames without reply but Taylor was not about to roll over and clawed his way back to 7-9 by the end of play on the first day. Incredibly, the scores were 11-11 as the match entered its final session and each time Davis edged in front Taylor would reel him back. Davis eked out a 17-15 lead but Taylor won the following two frames to level the game at 17 frames apiece with just one more to play.

That is where the encounter became nail-biting as Davis was leading 57-44 as the pair potted their way down to the colours. The reigning champion potted a long yellow and managed to bring the cue ball back into the baulk area but left himself a difficult shot on the green as a nervous Taylor could only watch. Davis neglected to take the pot but was extremely lucky that the pink ball lay between where the white and the green balls ended up.

Unruffled, Taylor screwed around the pink to leave the green near the side cushion where he felt it was safe, with the white on the opposite side of the table. Davis attempted a double into the corner but missed and was fortunate that the green came off three cushions to fall into the middle pocket in what is called a cocked-hat shot to give him an 18-point lead. He attempted to play a safety shot that would leave the white behind the black but over-hit the cue ball and it rebounded out from the cushion to leave a clear view of the brown. The frame had been underway for an incredible 55 minutes and none of the spectators could have imagined the drama that was about to unfold.

Taylor's long shot at the brown missed the pocket with the colour cannoning off the blue to end up reasonably safe on the side cushion. Although still potable, Davis rattled the jaws of the corner pocket to leave Taylor with a clear chance of sinking the brown but he too failed to add the four points to his score. He had, however, left the white and brown balls at opposite ends of the table. Davis again tried to leave the white behind the black ball but there was not enough power behind the brown and all the champion had done apart from move the black out from the cushion was to give the challenger another chance.

Taylor realised that it would be almost impossible to get into position for the blue so played a safety shot that left the chance of a pot for his opponent. Davis tried to slot the brown in the corner but missed and left the coloured ball up the baulk end of the table. It was now in a much better position for Taylor to take on the subsequent blue and he sank the four-point ball. He had over-hit the white slightly, however, which left him with a more difficult blue and less chance of an easy pink. He successfully cleared the pink but was now left with the cue ball on one side of the table with the black on the other.

Taylor tried a risky reverse double shot but was rewarded for his ambition when the white returned to the baulk area and the black bounced off the jaw of the middle pocket and ran to the other end of the table. There were just three points difference and each player knew that his first mistake would probably be his last. Davis played a safety shot that saw the two balls swap ends but Taylor went for the jugular with a double into the corner. Although he failed, he did leave the black fairly safe and lured Davis into a failed double with the two balls cannoning into each other to give Taylor a long shot to the corner.

Taylor took the bait but missed and left Davis a difficult pot into the corner. Many thought that Taylor had blown his chance but Davis over-cut the black to leave Taylor with the easiest of opportunities to claim the world title. As the black dropped into the pocket, the new world champion – with his trademark angled oversized glasses – raised his cue above his head in celebration.

JOE JOHNSON WINS THE WORLD TITLE AS 150-1 OUTSIDER 1986

Having won through to his fourth consecutive world championship final and with the memory of the previous year's final black defeat at the hands of Dennis Taylor (see page 30) fresh in his mind, Steve Davis took on the largely unknown Joe Johnson in the 1986 final. Davis, ranked number one in the world, was expected to make short shrift of the Yorkshireman despite the fact that he had played entertaining and attacking snooker throughout the tournament.

The 1986 competition was also notable for seeing the first outing of a future champion in 17-year-old Stephen Hendry who lost his first-round match against Willie Thorne by 10 frames to eight. One other notable name who was eliminated in the first round was reigning champion Dennis Taylor who lost 6-10 to Mike Hallett as the Crucible curse continued.

Joe Johnson had failed to win any match at the world championships in six attempts so few punters would have risked their hard-earned money on him to win…even at 150-1! Johnson won his first ever match at the Crucible and started his run to the final with a 10-3 demolition of Dave Martin before taking on Taylor's conqueror Hallett in the next round. Hallett proved to be no more of a stumbling block than Martin had and was dispatched 13-6.

Johnson's quarter-final opponent was much more experienced and posed a greater danger to his ambitions. Terry Griffiths had won the 1979 world title but had failed to fulfil his potential and had never progressed beyond the quarter-final stage in the intervening years. He was again destined to go out at this stage of the tournament, but he did put up a fight as Johnson won a fascinating encounter by 13-12 after trailing at 9-12.

Johnson was paired with Tony Knowles in the next round. The 30-year-old from Bolton was appearing in his third world championship semi-final and had shot to overnight fame when he trounced Steve Davis 10-1 in the first round of the 1982 tournament. This was the furthest that Knowles would ever progress in this competition and Johnson claimed a 16-8 victory.

Steve Davis, on the other hand, enjoyed a relatively comfortable ride through to the final beginning with a 10-4 first-round victory over Ray Edmonds. Doug Mountjoy provided the

opposition in the next round but Davis breezed past the Welshman by 13 frames to five to set up a quarter-final meeting with Jimmy White. The two had fought a thrilling encounter in the 1984 final with Davis narrowly winning by 18-16 but this time he registered a convincing 13-5 victory over White.

Davis met another of his world championship final victims in the semi-final when he was paired with Cliff Thorburn. The Canadian, however, was not able to reproduce the form that had brought him one trophy and two runners-up spots and was eliminated by a 16-12 scoreline.

Rather than be overawed by his opponent, Johnson took the game to Davis and continued playing the attacking snooker that had got him to the final. He opened up a 17-12 lead over the three-time champion and made no mistake as he claimed the 30th frame out of a possible 35 with a break of 64 to clinch the world title. Maybe it was because he came from nowhere to triumph over Davis that he became so popular with the British public or was it the "Bradford's bouncing back" T-shirt he wore between matches (a reference to the previous year's tragedy at Bradford City Football Club in which 56 fans died).

Joe Johnson was born in Bradford on 29 July 1952 and was one of the best amateurs in the early 1970s. He turned professional in 1979 but found success difficult to come by. It seemed that he lost his nerve when playing in front of the television cameras – although as an amateur he held the world record break of 140 that had been filmed – but won his first televised match at the 1985 Mercantile Credit Classic.

Davis and Johnson would again be paired in the 1987 final with the Yorkshireman aiming to become the first player to successfully defend his first Crucible title. Indeed, he was the only player who had even made it through to the final in the season after their first victory (1997 winner Ken Doherty also achieved this in 1998 when he lost 18-12 to John Higgins).

Johnson claimed the Scottish Masters title in 1987-88 but found himself dropping down the rankings and eventually retired in 2004. He had suffered from heart problems in the latter stages of his career and had experienced difficulty in coming to terms with having to wear glasses to play. He took teenage prodigy Paul Hunter under his wing and while he was elated at the youngster's hat-trick of Masters titles in the early 21st century the whole snooker community was devastated to hear of his death from cancer at the age of 27.

STEVE DAVIS COMPLETES A HAT-TRICK OF WORLD TITLES 1989

After having fallen at the last hurdle in 1985 and 1986, Steve Davis went on to claim a hat-trick of world titles in the last three years of the decade. He dominated the sport so much that the majority of the public would want his opponent to win no matter who they were (much like Manchester United in 1990s football).

Steve Davis – born on 22 August 1957 in Plumstead, London – was no relation to brothers Joe and Fred who won so much in the early years of the sport. He had already claimed numerous titles including three world championships (in 1981, 1983 and 1984) and was well on his way to becoming snooker's first millionaire.

His first obstacle in 1987 was Warren King but the American was quickly disposed of by a 10-7 scoreline. Next up was the veteran Ray Reardon who had won the championship six times in the 1970s. The Welshman was, however, no match for Davis and was thrashed by 13 frames to four. Terry Griffiths was his opponent in the quarter-final but the 1979 winner was convincingly beaten 13-5. The only man standing between Davis and a fifth successive final was Londoner Jimmy White who was a particular favourite of the British public with his quick and entertaining style of play. In a repeat of the 1984 final, Davis eliminated White – this time by 16 frames to 11 – to set up a meeting with reigning champion Joe Johnson.

Johnson – who had never won a match at the Crucible before the previous year's tournament – came through the earlier rounds with victories over Eugene Hughes (10-9), Murdo Macleod (13-7), Stephen Hendry (13-12) and Neal Foulds (16-9). He was unable to repeat his 1986 performance and lost to Davis – who had registered the highest break of the tournament with 132 – by 14-18.

The following year saw Davis paired with John Virgo in the opening round but the trick shot supreme made an early exit with a 10-8 defeat. Mike Hallett was next in the firing line and it certainly looked like an ambush as Davis registered a 13-1 victory and set his targets on Tony Drago. The Maltese player also exited with hardly a whimper in a 13-3 thrashing that set up a

repeat of the 1983 final against Cliff Thorburn. The Canadian proved a tougher nut to crack but Davis still disposed of him with consummate ease in a 16-8 semi-final win.

Terry Griffiths was Davis's opponent in the final and he had opened his account in that tournament with a 10-6 victory over Steve Longworth before ejecting Willie Thorne from the competition in a keenly fought 13-9 encounter. Neal Foulds (13-9) and Jimmy White (16-11) were dispatched at the quarter- and semi-final stages but Griffiths was unable to win his fifth consecutive match at the tournament. The Davis success story continued with an 18-11 triumph over the Welshman – despite the scores being tied at 8-8 after two sessions – as the adopted Essex boy claimed his fifth world title and a cheque for £95,000.

Steve Davis's hold on the world title was never really in any doubt during the 1989 competition. It seemed that no-one could compete with the winning machine as he recorded a 10-5 first-round victory over Steve Newbury. Steve Duggan and Mike Hallett were disposed of 13-3 each in the next two rounds and it looked like the up-and-coming Stephen Hendry might be able to give Davis a run for his money in the semi-final. As it turned out, the young Scotsman – who was the first from his country to make the semi-final since Walter Donaldson in the 1940s and 1950s – was beaten 16-9 but didn't leave empty-handed as he registered the highest break of the tournament with 141.

John Parrott won through to his first ever world championship final by recording wins over Steve James (10-9) and 1985 champion Dennis Taylor (13-10). Jimmy White was his quarter-final opponent but was unable to progress to the same stage of the competition as he had the previous year when Parrott won 13-7. It was a similar story in the semi-final when Tony Meo – with whom Davis had won four world doubles titles – could only manage to win seven frames in a best out of 31 match.

The final, however, proved to be the most one-sided in the history of the tournament since its 1969 relaunch. Davis registered an 18-3 victory that gave him a hat-trick of back-to-back world titles, his sixth in total that equalled Reardon's modern day achievement. Steve Davis was awarded the MBE in 1989 but his domination was about to be brought to an abrupt end by Stephen Hendry.

STEPHEN HENDRY, YOUNGEST EVER WORLD CHAMPION 1990

The new decade saw the arrival of a new star in a young Scotsman named Stephen Hendry. Although he had first entered the world championships at the tender age of 17 – when he predicted that he would win the event within five years – 1990 was the year he really came of age by becoming the youngest ever winner of the tournament. He eclipsed the achievement of Alex Higgins in 1972 and claimed the world title at just 21 years and three months old…a year ahead of schedule.

Stephen Hendry was born in Edinburgh on 13 January 1969 and quickly proved to be a sensation on the snooker table. He won the national under-16 championship in 1983 when he was just 14 years of age and amazed the audience of *Junior Pot Black* with his talent. The following year Hendry collected the Scottish amateur title and became the youngest ever competitor at the world amateur championships. He successfully defended his Scottish amateur title in 1986, the same year the 16-year-old turned professional. While it took many famous snooker stars years before they gained the confidence to give up their jobs and try their luck on the professional circuit, Stephen Hendry barely had time to leave school and adjust to life before he had taken the plunge.

The gamble paid off almost immediately as he began improving. He qualified for the last 32 of the Mercantile Credit Classic and made his first appearance at the Crucible, losing 8-10 to Willie Thorne before becoming the youngest ever winner of the Scottish Professional. The youngster finished his first season as a professional with a world ranking of 51.

But 1987-88 was the start of something special as Hendry claimed victory in that season's Grand Prix and the British Open, his first two rankings titles (he would go on to register 26 more ranking victories before the 1990s came to an end). He also scored a third successive Scottish Professional title to announce to the world that he was here to stay.

Although he failed to win any ranking tournaments in 1988-89, he did record his first victory in the Masters (a tournament he would dominate for the next five years) and moved up to number

three in the world rankings. The following season he claimed the UK Championship and headed east to triumph in the Dubai Duty Free Classic and the Asian Open. He added the Masters and the Scottish Masters and started the 1990 world championships as the favourite.

Hendry had begun his tournament with a first-round victory over Canada's Alain Robidoux, with the talented Scot registering a 10-7 winning margin. He met Tony Meo in the second round and eased past him by 13-7 to set up a quarter-final clash with Darren Morgan but the 23-year-old Welshman was unable to stop Hendry and went down 13-6. The ever-smiling John Parrott was his semi-final opponent but the Liverpudlian – who was ranked number two in the world – found Hendry too elusive and bowed out of the competition with an 11-16 defeat. Parrott did, however, have the consolation of scoring the biggest break in the tournament with 140.

Jimmy White had won his way through to the second world championship final of his career so far (he lost 16-18 to Steve Davis in 1984). Although he had eased past David Taylor (10-6), John Virgo (13-6) and Terry Griffiths (13-5) to get to the semi-final, there he met his nemesis in reigning champion Davis. It seemed that whenever there was a big occasion, White would be paired with Davis and the outcome nearly always signalled a victory for the adopted Essex boy. Not this time though, as White recorded a 16-14 victory that consigned Davis to his first defeat at the Crucible for four years.

Jimmy White – born on 2 May 1962 – was introduced to snooker by his father at the age of 11. He developed into a talented player and scored his first century the following year. He won the English amateur title in 1979, turned professional a year later and soon gained a huge following. Proving himself to be an extremely popular star, White was soon nicknamed "Whirlwind" because of the fast nature of his play, with an alternative moniker being the "people's champion".

The final itself proved to be an interesting encounter between a young man full of confidence and an experienced professional who had been in this sort of situation many times before. Hendry clinched the title with a break of 71 in the 30th frame that game him a convincing 18-12 victory. These two players would meet in the final three times over the next four years, with Hendry winning each one. Jimmy White was forever destined to be the bridesmaid as he never managed to claim that elusive world crown despite making six appearances in the final.

JIMMY WHITE, SECOND TO HIT 147 AT THE CRUCIBLE 1992

Perennial crowd favourite Jimmy White became only the second ever player to compile a maximum 147 break at the world championships held at the Crucible in 1992. The memorable event took place in the 13th frame of his first-round match with Tony Drago, with White in a commanding 8-4 lead in a best of 19 frame game.

The frame started with both players attempting safety shots as the reds became more and more spread out across the table. Drago went for a long pot that didn't come off and he left White with plenty of reds to decide from. On his day, Drago was a fearsome potter but he often took chances that many other players would have shied away from and on this occasion the gamble didn't pay off.

Having lost the previous two frames, White was taking it easy while regaining his composure. He potted his first red and could see that there were about four or five that he could quite easily pot with a black following each. He didn't quite get his position right after the third red and had to screw back after the black, narrowly missing the red that was next on the potting list. After his fifth red-black combination, White sent the cue ball into the pack of reds and split them with ease. It was now that he began to consider a possible 147 break a reality.

It's every player's ambition to record a 147 in a tournament and achieving this in the world championship is a dream come true. For them, it's not necessarily about the money, but the esteem that a maximum break brings. Gary Wilkinson had gone very close the previous year but had rattled the yellow in the jaws of the pocket.

White's positioning after potting his sixth black left a little to be desired so he had to play the next red with some right-hand side in order to get back onto the black. It wasn't all going to plan, however, and a little shake of the head indicated that he'd sent the cue ball slightly too far after potting his eighth black. A perfect shot on the next red though put him back in prime position to continue the break and he later explained that he doesn't just practice his shots but also concentrates on maintaining his composure.

JIMMY WHITE, SECOND TO HIT 147 AT THE CRUCIBLE

He aimed to open up the remaining few reds as he potted the black that took him to 80 points but all he succeeded in doing was nudging the pink out of the way. It necessitated a long shot up the table to pot the red that lay in the baulk area but the cue ball kissed a red on the way back to leave him a difficult shot on the black. The thought briefly crossed his mind about taking the easier pink instead and going for a 146 break but he quickly banished that idea and successfully potted the black.

After potting his 12th black, he tried to get position on both the reds that were still in the middle of the table and ended up with a difficult shot from behind the pink. He recovered but clipped the pink after sinking the red and ended up near the cushion. He was beginning to feel the tension but was too committed to the 147 to consider taking any colour other than the black.

A beautifully-paced shot on the 14th black allowed him to get into the right position to be able to pot the final red and take on the last black before heading back up the table for the yellow. With all the balls on their spots apart from the pink, the situation was looking good for White. There were no further heart-stopping moments, although the green did wobble slightly as it dropped into the corner pocket, and Jimmy White duly recorded his 147 break to claim the £100,000 prize for a maximum and a bear hug from Drago!

White won the next frame to go through to a second-round meeting with Alain Robidoux. Edging past the Canadian by 13-11, White then had more comfortable victories over Jim Wynch (13-9) and Alan McManus (16-7) before taking on Stephen Hendry in a repeat of the 1990 final.

Many critics say that the 1992 final was Jimmy White's best chance of winning the world championship. Leading at 12-6 and then 14-8, he was only a red and a subsequent colour away from winning the 23rd frame but allowed Hendry to come back into it when he missed the vital shot. Hendry, of course, took full advantage and won that frame and then the next nine – including breaks of 134 and 112 in the final two frames – to clinch an 18-14 victory and his second world title. White had also had chances to win the 24th and 25th frames when he was just one red away from registering a winning score but it was not to be for the "people's champion".

JOHN PARROTT, WHITEWASH AT THE CRUCIBLE
1992

It's not very often that experienced players get whitewashed and it's even rarer that it happens in the world championship final stages. But that's what happened in 1992 when John Parrott registered the only ever whitewash in the history of the tournament's final rounds with a 10-0 victory over Eddie Charlton.

The pair met in the first round of the tournament and Parrott – the reigning champion – could not have expected such an easy ride against Charlton, runner-up on three occasions between 1968 and 1975. This was not the only shock result of the first round as newcomer Peter Ebdon destroyed six-time world champion Steve Davis by 10-4 and Chris Small – an 18-year-old bank clerk from Edinburgh – triumphed 10-7 over 1981 finalist Doug Mountjoy. Ebdon would make his way through to the quarter-final where he lost against Terry Griffiths while Small's adventure ended with a second-round defeat at the hands of Dene O'Kane. Parrot himself, managed to win through to the quarter-finals but lost a thrilling encounter with Alan McManus by 12-13.

John Parrot was born in Liverpool on 11 May 1964 and showed early promise at bowls. His father, though, introduced his 12-year-old son to snooker on a wet day that laid the foundations for a spectacular career in the sport. Within four years, Parrott had made a 129 break and was runner-up in the national under-16 championship. He went on to win the Pontins junior title the following year and in 1982 lost to Neal Foulds in the national under-19s. He again won the Pontins Open and added the *Junior Pot Black* title to his resumé in 1982 and 1983 before reaching the final of the English amateur championship.

Parrott turned professional in 1983 and made his world championship debut the following year. After beating Tony Knowles 10-7 in the first-round, he lost his next match 11-13 against Dennis Taylor. But he had shown he was capable of beating some of the best professionals on the circuit and reached the quarter-final of the 1985 tournament, narrowly losing 12-13 to Ray Reardon, winner of six titles between 1970 and 1978. Three second-round exits followed – two at the hands of Jimmy White and once by Cliff Thorburn – and the 1987-88 season saw John Parrott firmly

JOHN PARROTT, WHITEWASH AT THE CRUCIBLE

ensconced in the top 16 of the world rankings, a position he consistently occupied for 14 years.

Parrott lost out to Steve Davis in the final of the Mercantile Credit Classic and Stephen Hendry in the B&H Masters but did triumph over Terry Griffiths to claim the European Open in 1988-89. That was also the season when he first made it through to the final of the world championships but he ended up on the wrong end of a 3-18 scoreline. The thrashing dished out by Steve Davis was the heaviest ever recorded in a Crucible final.

Parrott successfully defended his European title the following season and in 1991 improved on his best performance in the world championship by beating Jimmy White in the final to claim his one and only world crown. The likeable Liverpudlian got through the first round unscathed with a 10-6 victory over Nigel Gilbert before almost handing out a whitewash to Tony Knowles. Luckily, Knowles managed to win one frame before his opponent got to 13 in the best of 25-frame match.

Terry Griffiths was dispatched in the quarter-final with Steve Davis suffering a similar fate in the semi-final. Parrott took the first seven frames of the final and though White managed to pull himself back into the match he could not prevent his opponent from registering an 18-11 victory and a first world crown…something Jimmy White was still attempting to achieve.

John Parrott again won the European Open in 1996 but his tournament victories in recent years have been few and far between. He has successfully carved out an alternative career as a television personality, both as a commentator and a team captain on the BBC quiz show *A Question Of Sport*.

Eddie Charlton, born in New South Wales on 31 October 1929 was a veteran of the sport. He was a good all-round athlete and excelled at football, surfing, cricket and boxing (he carried the Olympic torch in 1956) but it was as a snooker player that he found worldwide fame. Charlton, a coal miner, turned professional in 1963 and reached the finals of the 1968, 1973 and 1975 world championships.

Charlton enjoyed greater success in the *Pot Black* competition, winning the title in 1972, 1973 and 1980 (the same year he was awarded the Order of Australia). He retired in 1995 and resigned his membership of the WPBSA after a dispute and died on 8 November 2004 from post-operative complications while on an exhibition tour of New Zealand.

JIMMY WHITE & STEPHEN HENDRY BATTLE TO LAST FRAME 1994

The 1990s saw four classic encounters between Stephen Hendry and Jimmy White in the final of the world championships. The first in 1990 saw Hendry win his first title at the age of 21 (see page 42), but their meeting in the 1994 tournament is probably the best example of two players at the peak of their game.

The first-round match between Cliff Thorburn and Nigel Bond gave an indication of the thrills and excitement that were to come. With the 1980 champion leading by nine frames to two, Bond staged an unbelievable comeback to win the match 10-9. He beat Terry Griffiths 13-8 in the second round before losing to Hendry by a similar scoreline in the quarter-final.

Hendry had already disposed of Surrinda Gill and Dave Harold in the first two rounds. Hendry had looked to be claiming the £100,000 prize for a maximum 147 against Gill after potting 15 reds and blacks but he missed a long shot for the yellow. Harold – a quarter-finalist the previous year – had won the Asian Open but proved little match for Hendry who won by 13-2.

Stephen Hendry had fallen in his hotel bathroom and had chipped a bone in his elbow. As a result, he rested his arm in a sling whenever he wasn't actually playing but the injury was noticeably hampering his playing as he won his quarter-final tie with Nigel Bond. His semi-final with Steve Davis proved to be close initially but Hendry established an advantage as the match wore on and eventually won 16-9.

Jimmy White struggled to find his form early in his first-round match but eased through with a 10-6 scoreline. He also had a chance at a 147 but missed after 14 reds and blacks. He played an effective game in the second round to see off Neal Foulds 13-10 before entertaining the crowd with some ambitious shots in the quarter-final against Ken Doherty which he won 13-10. White faced the inexperienced Darren Morgan in his semi-final and breezed through to a 16-8 victory.

JIMMY WHITE & STEPHEN HENDRY BATTLE TO LAST FRAME

This was Jimmy White's best ever chance of winning the world title as Stephen Hendry was trying to play through the pain barrier. Hendry showed great determination as he quickly established a 5-1 advantage but White clawed his way back into the match to lead 10-9. From that moment on, neither player managed to stretch their lead to more than two frames. In the final frame with the match tied at 17 frames and 24 points apiece, White was at the table.

He had already racked up a break of 16 but left himself a difficult shot to pot the next red. Using the rest and an extension on his cue, White – who was the perfect example of how to play using a rest – successfully sank the red and added the blue. He added another red-blue followed by a red, and looked perfectly composed and in control of the frame. The audience and the watching millions on television truly believed that this would be Jimmy White's year. Then, unbelievably, the normally dependable White rattled the black in the jaws of the corner pocket and allowed Hendry back on the table trailing by 24-37.

The defending champion, believing that White would clear up, had resigned himself to losing his title but gratefully received the charitable contribution and – with nerves of steel – made no mistake in the rest of the frame. It was agonising for White to have to watch his opponent and he sat in his chair shaking his head in disbelief. Hendry did have a wobble on the pink with two reds left but succeeded in clearing the table with a break of 58 to break White's heart and claim his fourth world title.

A dejected White left the table as his opponent took the acclaim from the crowd. He later commented that people still come up to him and ask him how he managed to miss that black but he just puts it down to nerves, admitting he rushed the shot.

"My job as a sportsman," Hendry later explained, "is to punish the mistakes that my opponent makes and Jimmy made the mistake and I went to the table and punished him for it. There's no room for feeling sorry for him… The next day when you read all the papers, you start to think that it is hard on him but I certainly don't feel sorry for him to the extent that I wish he'd won!"

Hendry went on to claim a further title in 1999 (see page 66) but for Jimmy White this was the last of his six appearances in the final. He had finished second-best in them all and his chance of winning the world championship had disappeared.

RONNIE O'SULLIVAN, FASTEST 147 IN 5 MIN 20 SECS 1997

Ronnie O'Sullivan had already made a name for himself since turning professional in 1992 but rewrote the history books in April 1997 when he compiled the fastest ever maximum 147 break at the world championships. In his first-round encounter with Mick Price, O'Sullivan was leading by eight frames to five in the best of 19-frame match but few could have foreseen how quickly the next frame would be won.

The 14th frame had started cautiously with both players attempting to play safety shots but with six reds already scattered from the pack, Price left O'Sullivan a longish shot to the corner. He took that shot with ease and quickly racked up a break of 56, sending the cue ball into the pack after his seventh red. As the break came up to the two minute 30 second mark, O'Sullivan had already established a 64-point lead.

After potting his 11th black, he eased the cue ball towards the reds and succeeded in separating two of them. That left just two reds in close proximity that he needed to worry about but he split them after his next black to leave a perfect shot into the middle to achieve 97 points so far. The remaining three reds were each followed by blacks in quick succession as O'Sullivan reached the century in four minutes.

He left himself the perfect angle on the black after potting the last red and the cue ball traversed the table to line up for the yellow. The colours were disposed of with consummate ease and Ronnie O'Sullivan duly completed his 147 maximum. Each shot had been played to perfection and O'Sullivan had not taken any time between shots to really think about his game plan. The whole break had taken just five minutes and 20 seconds from potting the first red to sinking the final black to claim the £147,000 cheque for a maximum break.

While Price countered by taking the 15th frame, O'Sullivan made sure of his progression to the second round by winning the subsequent frame to record a 10-6 victory. Such a great achievement showed that O'Sullivan was on top of his game and it would

RONNIE O'SULLIVAN, FASTEST 147 IN 5 MIN 20 SECS

RONNIE O'SULLIVAN, FASTEST 147 IN 5 MIN 20 SECS

have been interesting to see what he produced later in the tournament. Sadly, this was not to be as Darren Morgan ended his dream of a first world title in the next round. The Welshman won by the odd frame in 25 to clinch a place in the quarter-final where he lost to Stephen Hendry.

Hendry was unable to extend his run of title successes to cover five consecutive years when he faced Ken Doherty in the final. The match was a yo-yo affair with the Irishman establishing a 12-7 lead before going on to take the next three frames. The defending champion came back to win the next five frames to bring the score to 15-12 but Doherty claimed three more to win the title.

Ronnie O'Sullivan was born on 5 December 1975 in Chigwell and had taken up snooker at a very early age. When he was just 10 years old, he was entertaining audiences and registered a 117 break. He increased his best break score to 142 just two years later and won the British under-16 title the following year. Although he failed to successfully defend this title, he did reach the quarter-finals of the under-19 event.

His first maximum break came when he was just 15 years and 97 days old in the 1991 English amateur championship where he finished runner-up and he has since managed this feat a further five times. O'Sullivan turned professional the following year and entered his first world championships in 1993. Unfortunately, he failed to get past Alan McManus who registered a 10-7 victory.

O'Sullivan won his first professional title with the 1993 Nescafé Extra Challenge and added the UK championship before the year was out. He defeated two world champions in Steve Davis (9-6 in the quarter-final) and Stephen Hendry (10-6 in the final) to become the youngest winner of any ranking tournament at 17 years old. (Hendry got his revenge with a 9-5 victory in the following year's European Open final but O'Sullivan recovered to claim the British Open title with a 9-4 triumph over James Wattana.

Although he failed to win a ranking tournament in 1994-95, O'Sullivan did claim his first Masters title with a 9-3 victory against John Higgins the following season. He had eased through the earlier rounds with wins against Nigel Bond, Hendry and Peter Ebdon on his way to collect a cheque for £120,000.

O'Sullivan reached the next two Masters finals but lost to Davis and Hendry but won further titles in the German Open and Asian Classic prior to arriving at the Crucible where his best previous showing had been a semi-final appearance in 1996.

STEVE DAVIS, LAST MAJOR TOURNAMENT TITLE 1997

When Steve Davis claimed his third Masters title in 1997, there can't be many people who can hold their hand on their heart and say that they knew this would be his last major tournament victory. Although he had seen his dominance of the world snooker scene usurped by Stephen Hendry, Davis was still one of the best players on the circuit and it wasn't until 1999-2000 that he dropped out of the top 16 in world rankings.

It is true that his title successes greatly reduced in numbers in the 1990s and his last appearance in the world championship final had been back in 1989 when he trounced John Parrott (see page 38). Since that last victory, the closest he had come to the final was in 1990 when he lost 16-14 to Jimmy White. He again went out at the semi-final stage the following year, this time by a 16-10 scoreline against eventual winner Parrott and lost by 9-16 to Stephen Hendry in 1994.

He suffered the ignominy of going out in the first round in 1992 – with Peter Ebdon inflicting a 4-10 defeat (Ebdon also evicted him from the 1996 championship at the quarter-final stage) – and 1995 (7-10 against Andy Hicks) but made the second round in 1993 where he lost 11-13 to Alan McManus.

Davis had fared no better in the Benson & Hedges Masters either. His two trophies were claimed in 1982 with a 9-5 victory over Terry Griffiths and 1988 when he handed out a 9-0 whitewash to Mike Hallett. Apart from those two years, Davis never graced the final. In fact, it's a good thing that Davis did win the 1997 Masters otherwise the record books would have his last major tournament win as far back as 1989.

Of course, he did win minor events but many critics had written him off saying he was over the hill. His best year of the 1990s was in 1992 when he triumphed 9-8 over Stephen Hendry to win the Mercantile Credit Classic and beat Alan McManus to win the Asian Open before registering his second British Open title the following year with a 10-2 trouncing of James Wattana. He claimed four Irish Masters titles between 1990 and 1994,

GREATEST MOMENTS OF SNOOKER

two Regal Welsh Opens (1994-95) and two *Pot Black* crowns (1991 and 1993). He also claimed a hat-trick of world trickshot titles between1994-97.

The preliminary round of the 1997 Masters saw the first appearance in the tournament of Paul Hunter who was given a wildcard entry but lost 1-5 to Mark Williams. Hunter would go on to win the title three times between 2001 and 2004 before his untimely death in October 2006 at the age of 27.

Steve Davis started his 1997 Masters tournament with a 6-4 victory over Alan McManus before a second-round meeting with old foe Peter Ebdon who was also defeated by the same scoreline. Ken Doherty – the man who would go on to claim the world title in a couple of months' time – was Davis's semi-final opponent but he was easily dispatched 6-1 to put him through to his third final.

Ronnie O'Sullivan had seen off the challenge of Dave Harold with a 6-1 win in the first round before taking on archrival Stephen Hendry in the quarter-final. It proved a closely-fought encounter but the Englishman triumphed over the Scot by six frames to four to set up a meeting with Nigel Bond. The semi-final proved to be even closer, with O'Sullivan pipping Bond to the winning post in the deciding frame.

The final itself will be best remembered for the quality of snooker on display. O'Sullivan had established a 4-2 advantage during the afternoon session before Davis claimed the final two frames to level the tie. O'Sullivan was more focused by the evening session and quickly ran up a four-frame lead. Davis, however, began to put together some consistency and won six frames in a row to take the title by 10-8. In the penultimate frame, he had even put together a break of 139 that eclipsed O'Sullivan's 120 to also pocket the £15,000 for the highest break.

O'Sullivan later admitted that his concentration had been disrupted by an intruder in the arena when Lianne Crofts became the sport's first streaker. It obviously didn't bother Steve Davis though…

Ronnie O'Sullivan went on to appear in four consecutive finals between 2004 and 2007, claiming two further Masters titles. Having lost 9-10 to Paul Hunter in the first, the second was a repeat of the 1995 final and he emerged victorious by a 10-3 margin against John Higgins. Higgins however got his revenge with a 10-9 triumph in 2006 while O'Sullivan beat Ding Junhui 10-3 in 2007.

STEPHEN HENDRY WINS A RECORD SEVENTH WORLD TITLE 1999

There were a lot of critics and fans alike who were querying whether the Hendry bubble had burst. After winning five consecutive world titles between 1992-96 to add to his first in 1990, the 1998 final had proved to be only the second in the 1990s that Stephen Hendry did not contest. It didn't help either that he had been the victim of a first-round 9-0 whitewashing in the 1998 UK championship at the hands of fellow countryman Marcus Campbell.

Hendry's world championship began with an encounter with Paul Hunter. He managed to fend off the challenge of the rising star and registered a 10-8 victory to take him through to the second round. There he met James Wattana but the Thai player (born with the name Ratchapol Pu-Ob-Orm) was unable to prevent Hendry from triumphing by 13 frames to seven.

His opponent in the quarter-finals was Matthew Stevens and the six-time world champion soon established a 5-0 lead. Although the Welshman clawed two frames back, Hendry took the next three to establish an 8-2 advantage. The Scot won the 17th and 18th frames with breaks of 104 and 78 to emerge triumphant with a 13-5 scoreline.

The semi-final paired Hendry with Ronnie O'Sullivan and proved to be an entertaining match. Hendry was out of the starting blocks quicker than his opponent and, with a 126 break as the game began, took six out of the first seven frames. O'Sullivan then found his feet and claimed the next five frames – including breaks of 122 and 135 – to level the match at 6-6. Hendry managed to open up a three-frame advantage at 10-7 but by the end of the 24th it was all square.

O'Sullivan rattled off a 134 break to take the lead for the first – and what would prove to be the only – time in the match at 13-12 but Hendry went on to win the next five frames to clinch the match 17-13 and his place in the final.

Mark Williams' first two opponents were disposed of without too much concern with Ian McCulloch (10-4) and Nick Walker (13-7) warming him up nicely for his quarter-final clash with Ken Doherty. Although Doherty won the first frame, Williams soon established an 8-1 lead

STEPHEN HENDRY WINS A RECORD SEVENTH WORLD TITLE

that the 1997 champion found too difficult to overcome. He did close the gap to 5-9 and 7-11 but a 97 break from Williams in the 22nd frame gave the Welshman a place in the semi-final against defending champion John Higgins.

Higgins took the first frame but then Williams would pull a frame ahead only for his opponent to level the score. Higgins did take the lead briefly with a 127 break in the 15th frame that gave him an 8-7 advantage but could only win two more frames while Williams registered nine to win through to his first final.

The final started off with Hendry claiming the first four frames without reply with breaks of 62, 98 and 77. Williams responded by claiming three out of the next four but was not racking up the number of substantial breaks that his opponent was. Hendry won the 12th frame with a break of 132 to restore his four-frame advantage but would not be able to claim the highest break prize as John Higgins had already registered a 142.

And that is how the match progressed; Hendry would pull out in front and Williams would reel him back in. After the Welshman had clawed his way back to 8-6, Hendry won the next two frames to re-establish his four-frame lead. Williams took the next two with breaks of 85 and 72 and by the 20th frame was just 9-11 behind. Hendry, though, won the next six frames – including a 106 break in the 21st – to open up an eight-frame gap and leave himself just one frame away from his seventh world title.

Williams scored an 89 break in the 27th frame and pulled another back before giving Hendry the opportunity to clear up in the 29th with eight reds on the table and 16-40 down. Hendry – having spent much of the year working on his technique and concentration – calmly set about clearing the table and scored a break of 88 to claim the trophy despite missing the pink and almost knocking the black into the corner pocket. He also pocketed the tournament's biggest ever prize in the form of a £230,000 cheque.

Stephen Hendry went down in history as the greatest snooker player of the modern era with this victory. His seventh title eclipsed the achievements of Ray Reardon (1970s) and Steve Davis (1980s) who had each won the trophy six times and it is unlikely that this record will be matched or broken in the near future. The next generation of stars such as Ronnie O'Sullivan and Mark Williams have yet to demonstrate the consistency shown by the Scot and so lag far behind Hendry in terms of world title wins.

PAUL HUNTER'S AMAZING COMEBACK IN THE MASTERS 2001

The final session of the 2001 Masters tournament proved to be memorable in more ways than one. First, because of Paul Hunter's amazing comeback from 3-7 down and second because of the publicly aired reason for the revival in his fortunes.

The tournament was also notable for the absence of Steve Davis who had dropped out of the world's top 16 rankings. He was denied a wildcard entry that went instead to local favourite Jimmy White who repaid that faith when he beat Joe Swail 6-1 in the first round. The 1984 winner then faced the incomparable Ronnie O'Sullivan in the next round and easily disposed of the youngster by six frames to two.

White then found himself up against his archrival Stephen Hendry. The two had met in four consecutive world championship finals in the early 1990s with the young Scot winning them all. Sadly for White, this time was no exception as Hendry triumphed 6-4.

Paul Hunter was born in Leeds on 14 October 1978. His dad gave his three-year-old son a snooker table for Christmas and a rare talent was soon uncovered. He practiced as much as he could and, having dropped out of school two years earlier, turned professional in mid-1995 at the age of 16.

Hunter won his first tournament in 1998 at the Welsh Open but could not get past the semi-final at the Liverpool Victoria UK championship as he was named the Snooker Writers' Association's Young Player of the Year. With Hunter only breaking into the world's top 16 in 1999, his Masters record so far had seen him lose 3-6 to John Parrott in 2000 in his only appearance at the event.

Paul Hunter's 2001 tournament saw him kick off against close friend and defending champion Matthew Stevens in a tense opener. The Welshman put up a brave fight but lost 5-6 as Hunter went on to face Peter Ebdon in the quarter-final. Hunter had no problem overcoming that obstacle, however, and lined up in the semi-final against Stephen Hendry. The Scot had dominated the sport during the 1990s, winning seven world titles, but such was the talent of the

PAUL HUNTER'S AMAZING COMEBACK IN THE MASTERS

new generation of professionals that Hendry's star was on the wane. Hunter registered a reasonably comfortable 6-3 victory to send himself through to his first major final.

Fergal O'Brien's route to the final saw him take on reigning world champion Mark Williams in the second round. In a tense encounter, O'Brien emerged triumphant by 6-5 to win through to a quarter-final meeting with fellow Irishman Ken Doherty. The 1997 world titleholder was unable to stop O'Brien's charge though and was swept aside by a 3-6 scoreline. Ireland's sole representative in the semi-final duly dispatched England's Dave Harold to win 6-4 and book his place in the final.

In the final itself, O'Brien narrowly claimed the first two frames before Hunter got off the mark but then went on to win the next five to establish a 5-1 lead. Each player then won another frame apiece to go into the interval with the Irishman leading 6-2. Hunter's manager suggested that he try Plan B which stood for "bonk" but the Yorkshireman wasn't in the mood.

"Sex was the last thing on my mind," he later explained. "But I had to do something to break the tension. It was a quick session – around 10 minutes or so – but I felt great afterwards. (Girlfriend Lindsey) jumped in the bath, I had a kip and then played like a dream."

Hunter returned to the arena a rejuvenated man and went on to win two out of the first three frames of the session. He then recorded breaks of 129 and 101 to reduce the deficit to 6-7 before O'Brien won another frame. A break of 75 again brought Hunter to within one frame of his opponent before he registered the highest break of the tournament with a 136 that levelled the scores at 8-8.

O'Brien broke in the next frame and then had to be content to watch as Hunter cleared the table for a 132 to take the lead for the first time in the match. O'Brien did restore parity but Hunter won the final frame 77-44 to claim his first Masters title.

Afterwards, Hunter couldn't believe the media furore that followed his admission about what had happened during the interval. "I would never have guessed in a million years that I'd be on the front pages of four national newspapers and on breakfast television the next morning," he claimed. "The country went crazy. I just think it's funny."

Paul Hunter went on to retain his Masters title the following year and won a third title in 2004 before his tragic death in October 2006. The Snooker Writers' Association have since paid tribute to the memory by renaming its Newcomer of the Year award in his honour.

KEN DOHERTY, 15-9 DOWN, BEATS PAUL HUNTER
2003

There can be few who would argue that the semi-final of the 2003 world championships between Paul Hunter and Ken Doherty is one of the most exciting matches that have taken place in recent years. Although he lost the chance to go through to the final, Hunter contributed to the spectacle and it is a tragedy that he is not around to create any more moments of magic.

Hunter won through to the final with victories over Ali Carter (10-5) and best friend Matthew Stevens (10-6) before facing Peter Ebdon in the quarter-final. In a tense encounter, Hunter was able to emerge victorious over the reigning champion by 13-12. Doherty, on the other hand, faced tough matches of his own and only just managed to beat Shaun Murphy 10-9 in the first round. He had another close call in the second round, this time defeating Graeme Dott 13-12 before an "easier" quarter-final against John Higgins which the Irishman won 13-8.

Ronnie O'Sullivan, meanwhile, found out that the old adage about a 147 winning you only one frame was true. He became the first player to register a second maximum at the tournament, this one in his first-round match against Marco Fu but still went out with a 6-10 defeat.

The semi-final saw Hunter open up a 15-9 overnight lead by playing some of the best snooker the tournament had seen. Doherty won the first two frames of the final session and Hunter – at 62-36 up in the 27th with just the colours to clear – seemed to be showing signs of tension when he missed a relatively simple yellow. Hunter managed to slow the Doherty juggernaut and claimed the 30th frame to go 16-14 in front with just three to play but the Irishman won the remaining three frames to win 17-16.

"I only needed to win two out of the last nine," Hunter later explained. "I was so relaxed that it wasn't a case of me choking. I didn't have much luck and everything seemed to go Ken's way. I then won a frame to go 16-14 up. Ken won one back and then another. 16-16. But I still felt good. I got in first, but then ran out of position. Ken cleaned up and I missed the final."

Doherty went on to meet Mark Williams – winner of the 2000 tournament – in the final but lost 16-18 to the Welshman. The Irishman finished the competition having played 132 frames

KEN DOHERTY, 15-9 DOWN, BEATS PAUL HUNTER

out of a possible 137, the record for a single world championship but had no trophy to show for it.

Hunter was "devastated not to be in the final. For a couple of days I could do nothing. It was terrible – but then I watched the last few frames of the final and saw Ken just miss out. I knew I'd survive then!

"But I'm now desperate to be world champion…I will be world champion one day."

Sadly, this prediction would not come true as Hunter returned to the Crucible the following year but went out in the second round to Welshman Matthew Stevens. Despite leading 10-6 and then 12-10, Hunter was unable to claim the decisive frame and Stevens went on to clinch the match 13-12. In 2005 he lost his first-round match 8-10 to Michael Holt while his 5-10 defeat at the hands of Neil Robertson the following year would prove to be his last match as a professional.

Hunter had been diagnosed with malignant neuroendocrine tumours in March 2005. He suffered a lot while receiving chemotherapy treatment for this rare form of stomach cancer and although he bravely continued playing his world ranking position plummeted because of the pain he was in. The WPBSA announced in July 2006 that a members' vote had brought about a rule change so that Hunter could take the 2006-07 season off to fight his illness with his world ranking frozen at number 34. Unfortunately, Hunter would never return to the table and it was announced on 9 October 2006 that he had lost his fight for life in a hospice in Huddersfield.

His fellow professionals were quick to pay tribute with seven-time world champion Stephen Hendry admitting "I'm absolutely devastated by the news. He's got a young family and he had a fantastic future in front of him. It's everyone's worst nightmare and puts everything into perspective."

Following Paul Hunter's death, Jimmy White led the campaign for the Masters trophy to be renamed in his honour. His widow Lindsey also pushed for the accolade, claiming "…everybody expected it. Every player I've spoken to, every fan, thought it would be a definite." But the sport's ruling body refused, stating that their Paul Hunter Scholarship – aimed at helping gifted youngsters fulfill their talent – was the most appropriate tribute.

RONNIE O'SULLIVAN THRASHES STEPHEN HENDRY 2004

Ronnie O'Sullivan and Stephen Hendry have had some epic encounters over the years but none have been so one-sided as the 2004 world championship semi-final. It's not just the end result that demoralises opponents, it's the speed at which it happens as well.

Nicknamed "Rocket" Ronnie, O'Sullivan has registered six maximum 147 breaks during his professional career and five of them just so happen to be the fastest on record. He scored his first maximum at the 1997 world championships, a feat he repeated at the 2003 tournament. He has also notched up 147 at the 1999 Welsh Open, the 1999 Grand Prix, the 2000 Scottish Regal Open and the 2001 LG Cup.

O'Sullivan had already won the world title three years earlier when he beat John Higgins by 18-14. He also won the UK championship the same year along with the Irish Masters (he first won this title in 1998 with a 9-3 victory over Ken Doherty but was disqualified after failing a drugs test) and China International tournaments. He claimed the regal Scottish Masters three times between 1998 and 2002 and was ranked number one in the world going to the Crucible.

O'Sullivan had a new mentor in the form of Ray Reardon, who had won six world titles in the 1970s. He was full of praise for the new addition to his backroom team saying "I'm more excited about working with Ray than I am about winning the world title. Thanks to him I feel I can just get better and better."

His opponents will be hoping that that just isn't physically possible after the way he demolished everyone who stood in his way at the Crucible. O'Sullivan began the tournament with a 10-6 victory over Stephen Maguire before facing Andy Hicks in the second round. The 26-year-old from Devon had nearly caused a fight after his first-round 10-4 triumph over Quinten Hann. The Australian took offence when Hicks pointed out that he would more than likely drop out of the world's top 16 after losing the match…

Hann wasn't the only player to display an outburst of temper as O'Sullivan himself expressed anger and dismay at his performance in the opening rounds. He was, however, far enough on top

of his game to see off the challenge of Hicks. It was a close shave, though, and it took O'Sullivan all of his experience to win 13-11.

O'Sullivan found his form in the quarter-final and disposed of Anthony Hamilton 13-3 to set up an encounter with Stephen Hendry. Unusually, the Scot was not playing to his usual standards and O'Sullivan breezed past the seven-time world champion by 17 frames to four to book his place in the final against Graeme Dott.

Dott also found that his winning margins were rather narrower than he might have hoped for. His first-round match against Mark King went right down to the wire but he scraped through by 10-9 to meet fellow Scot John Higgins in the next round. The 1998 champion and 2001 runner-up was dispatched by 13-10 and Dott looked forward to his quarter-final against David Gray. This was the most comfortable of his victories, as he eased through to a semi-final with Matthew Stevens with a winning score of 13-7. The match was another tense affair, but Dott triumphed in the end and registered a 17-15 win.

Graeme Dott stunned the audience and O'Sullivan by running up a 5-0 lead in the final, with breaks of 71 and 77 in the first two frames. O'Sullivan responded, however, by taking the next four frames…the first with an even century break. A break of 77 in the 12th brought the scores level but Dott registered an 86 to edge in front again. O'Sullivan retaliated with five frames on the trot before Dott registered a 106 break to reduce the deficit to 8-11. As it turned out, that was the last frame the Scot would win as O'Sullivan went on to claim the seven he needed to win the match, scoring breaks of 85 and 92 along the way.

After the tournament, a confident O'Sullivan declared "I never thought I was going to lose. In fact I thought I was going to win it before I came to Sheffield. I had rehearsed it in my mind and I was convinced about what would happen. I'd like to win more world titles, possibly four or five. You've got to set yourself high standards to stay motivated."

Only time will tell whether Ronnie O'Sullivan can equal Stephen Hendry's record of seven world titles but no-one can deny that he certainly has the talent – if not always the temperament – to do so.

MARK WILLIAMS, FIRST WELSH 147 AT THE CRUCIBLE 2005

As Ronnie O'Sullivan found out in 2003, a 147 maximum break does not guarantee winning a match. But it does if it happens when the player only needs one more frame for victory as Mark Williams discovered in his first-round match against Robert Milkins at the 2005 world championships when he registered his first ever maximum in tournament play.

As the match entered its 11th frame, Williams was leading by 9-1 and stepped up to break. He split the pack nicely but left the cue ball reasonably safe in the baulk area. With nothing to lose, Milkins attempted a long pot into the corner but missed, allowing Williams the opportunity to begin building a break.

The twice world champion successfully potted his first red and proceeded to add a black before clearing up the remaining loose reds. After sinking his fourth black, Williams left himself an angle to go into the pack but the contact was slightly thinner than intended and – although the reds did split reasonably well, the white rolled up towards the middle pocket and made the following shot more difficult than it perhaps should have been. He again sent the white into the pack after his sixth red-black combination to perfectly scatter the reds and make the possibility of a 147 more realistic.

Williams left himself a bit short of position after the eighth black and, with the pink blocking a red into the middle pocket, decided to play for a red that left him a more difficult black into the corner. Luckily for Williams, it was the best side of the table for him as a left-hander and he sank the black with the cue ball running the length of the table to clear the rogue red that had ended up in the baulk area. He potted the red in the corner but needed to force an angle to regain position on the black. Unfortunately, the white ended up very close to the black leaving Williams with a difficult shot to keep on track for his 147. Having to use the rest, Williams succeeded in sinking the black with a very fine cut and the cue ball nestled perfectly in position to resume the break on 80.

He cleared the remaining reds and left the perfect angle on the black to set his sights on the yellow. All the colours were on their respective spots apart from the pink which was slightly to one

MARK WILLIAMS, FIRST WELSH 147 AT THE CRUCIBLE

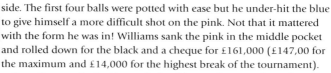

side. The first four balls were potted with ease but he under-hit the blue to give himself a more difficult shot on the pink. Not that it mattered with the form he was in! Williams sank the pink in the middle pocket and rolled down for the black and a cheque for £161,000 (£147,00 for the maximum and £14,000 for the highest break of the tournament).

Tony Drago, who had been playing his own first-round match against Stephen Lee on the next table, had been watching the events unfold and soon came to congratulate Williams on his remarkable achievement. He added his name to the roll of honour with the sixth 147 maximum break at the world championships after Cliff Thorburn (1983), Jimmy White (1992), Stephen Hendry (1995) and Ronnie O'Sullivan (1997 and 2003). He was the first Welshman to achieve this.

Then coached by Terry Griffiths – who had been in the commentary box during his charge's fascinating final frame – Mark Williams had come into the tournament looking to regain his position as world number one and he got off to the perfect start (he had been ranked the world's best player in the 2000-01, 2001-02 and 2003-04 seasons). His participation in the event did not last long, however, as he found himself losing to Ian McCulloch in the next round. The Lancastrian won a closely fought encounter that went right down to the wire and emerged with a 13-12 victory to end Williams' dreams of a third title for yet another season.

Awarded the MBE in 2004 – the same year he became a father – Williams suffered a short barren spell in the mid-2000s but returned to winning ways with a thrilling 9-8 victory over John Higgins in the final of the 2006 China Open. It was his first ranking tournament win in over two years and helped him return to the top 10. Williams managed to reach the quarter-final of that year's world championship but narrowly lost to Ronnie O'Sullivan by 11-13.

Williams – who sometimes has to ask the referee to confirm whether a ball is red or black because of his eyesight – claimed the Pot Black trophy in late 2006 but went out of the 2007 UK championships in the third round to eventual runner-up Stephen Hendry with a 6-9 defeat.

DING JUNHUI, FIRST FOREIGNER TO WIN UK CHAMPIONSHIP 2005

Ding Junhui was born on 1 April 1987 in Yixing, Jiangsu near Shanghai. He began playing snooker aged nine and to this day still practises his game for around eight hours each day. He is the top snooker player in China and for the snooker season resides in the UK. He became a professional in 2003 and quickly established himself as a serious contender for the most distinguished snooker accolades.

The 2005 Travis Perkins UK championship was hosted at the Barbican Centre in York from 5-18 December. In round one Junhui was faced with Anthony Hamilton whom he defeated comfortably in a 9-3 victory. His fellow finalist Steve Davis was happily beating Mark Allen 9-7 in the second round before meeting Scotland's Stephen Maguire in round three. Davis won by one frame (9-8) while Junhui fought his way through round two with a 9-3 victory over Jimmy White. He then met Paul Hunter in round three whom he comfortably defeated 9-2. The quarter-finals saw Junhui see off Neil Robertson from Australia 9-5 while Davis made it through to the next round with a 9-7 victory over Irishman Ken Doherty. In the semi-finals it was Junhui against Joe Perry. The result was 9-4 in favour of the Chinese contender while Davis played Stephen Hendry in a comfortable 9-6 triumph.

The scene was set for the final and it pitted Junhui against the more experienced Davis. At only 18 years of age, Junhui was the first non-British or Irish winner of the prestigious UK title when he defeated the veteran former champion by 10-6. Junhui looked strong from the start and Davis was trailing 5-3 by the interval. He fought back at the beginning of the evening session but Junhui proved a strong opponent. Davis – a six times world champion – was playing his 100th career final but even he found it tough going against the young outsider.

Junhui managed to match Davis and was the stronger player on the day when he triumphed with a 10-6 victory over his more senior rival. His positional play proved inspiring and he was not fazed by the shots that Davis dealt. He remained strong and confident throughout the match and Davis could be seen supporting the young player from China with his appreciation of Junhui's

stance on the game. During the third frame Junhui was consistent in his pressure shots to clinch frames and he scored 111 – the highest break of the match. Davis meanwhile was struggling to make good positions after his shots.

After he had clinched the title, Ding Junhui spoke through an interpreter to thank the spectators for their support. Many of the crowd were pro-Davis supporters but all rallied round to encourage the youngster who went on to say through his interpreter that: "This is the second most important ranking tournament so it is a great pleasure to win it."

Ding Junhui had won the China Open earlier in 2005 but wasn't expected to be in contention for the UK championship. Since his win, former champions – including Ronnie O'Sullivan and Stephen Hendry – have voiced their predictions that Ding Junhui is a formidable player who is one to watch for the next 10 to 15 years. He has received considerable high praise from those who are snooker's heroes and his impact on the game has been massive. The teenager is already a sporting hero in his native China and sponsorship deals are being offered thick and fast while China is waking up to the idea of snooker as an enjoyable sport. As the world of snooker has been dominated by the UK and Ireland since time began, Junhui's success has meant that he has become an icon watched by millions. Junhui's career has been backed by his family who have borrowed a great deal of money to finance his meteoric rise.

Ding Junhui's professional career took off when, presented with a wildcard to enter the Masters tournament in London, he defeated Joe Perry who was ranked 16th in the world. He narrowly missed winning over Stephen Lee when he lost by one frame in a 6-5 victory to Lee. In the 2005 China Open, he defeated Peter Ebdon, Marco Fu and Ken Doherty and Stephen Hendry (who faced Junhui in the final) to win the championship by 9-5. It was Junhui's first ranking tournament. He moved from 60th in the world rankings to 31st as a result of his UK championship win which then meant that Junhui automatically qualified for various prestigious tournaments in future. In the summer of 2006 he successfully defeated Ronnie O'Sullivan to win the Northern Ireland Trophy by 9-6 and his world ranking went to number five. At the end of 2006 Junhui won three gold medals at the Asian Games and reached the quarter-final of the UK championship but lost to Peter Ebdon nine frames to five. In January 2007 he defeated Cao Xinlong by 5-4 to play in the Chinese National Snooker final which he won, beating Xiao Guodong 6-2.

GRAEME DOTT & PETER EBDON, LONGEST FRAME 2006

The 2006 world championships – with 888.com taking over sponsorship of the event from Embassy – saw the longest ever frame to be played at the Crucible when it took Graeme Dott and Peter Ebdon 74 minutes to decide the winner of the 27th frame. It eventually finished with Ebdon reducing the deficit to just three frames after a score of 66-59.

The final began with both players being very cautious and as a result only six frames were played in the first session. Ebdon took the first with a break of 63 but lost the second despite scoring 52 points in one visit to the table. Dott then claimed the next three frames before his opponent rallied with a 61 break to finish the session at 4-2. The break in play was obviously beneficial to Dott as he took the next four frames to establish an 8-2 lead and by midway point he had stretched his advantage to seven frames at 12-5.

Ebdon took the 18th frame with a break of 78 and added the 19th before his opponent then rattled off another three-frame salvo that took him to within three frames of the finishing post. The 2002 champion retaliated with a break of 117 in the 23rd and went on to claim the next five frames – including the 28th in a speedy 11 minutes – to reduce the deficit to just 13-15. Dott registered a break of 66 to go 16-13 up (after his opponent had conceded the frame having gone in-off) and though Ebdon won the next frame his opponent claimed the final two he needed to win the match. Before potting the final ball, Dott went over and kissed the famous trophy as he won his first professional tournament. The final finished at 12.53am, making it the latest finish for a final in the venue's history.

Dott's route to the final saw him see off the first-round challenge of John Parrott. The 1991 champion was easily disposed off with a 10-3 scoreline. His next opponent was Nigel Bond but the 1996 British Open winner was unable to extend his stay in the tournament and Dott progressed to the quarter-final courtesy of a 13-9 victory. His opponent was Neil Robertson and the Australian battled hard with Dott clinching the deciding frame in a 13-12 success.

GRAEME DOTT & PETER EBDON, LONGEST FRAME

Dott was also involved in a thrilling semi-final clash with former champion Ronnie O'Sullivan. With the first session ending 5-3 in O'Sullivan's favour, the second session saw a reversal of fortunes that ended with the match tied at eight frames apiece. The Scotsman then embarked on an unstoppable sequence that saw him claim all eight frames of the next session. O'Sullivan staged a mini revival, taking the first three frames after the break but Dott then won the crucial frame he needed to take him through to the final.

Graeme Dott was born in Glasgow on 12 May 1977 and turned professional in 1994. He made his entry into the world's top 16 seven years later and has been a fixture there ever since. Prior to his world title success, Dott had only ever managed to become runner-up at the Regal Scottish Open (1999), the British Open (2001) and the Malta Cup (2005) and registered a competitive 147 maximum at the 1999 British Open.

He was also runner-up at the 2004 world championships when he lost 8-18 in the final to Ronnie O'Sullivan who was claiming his second title. Dott had reached that final with the aid of a new cue, having allegedly smashed his previous one to pieces at a motorway services on the M6 three months earlier.

Peter Ebdon was born in Kettering on 27 August 1970 and began playing snooker almost as soon as he entered his teens. He turned professional in 1991 and two years later registered his first ranking tournament title with the Skoda Grand Prix. This was followed by non-ranking tournament victories in the Irish Masters, the Malta Grand Prix and the Scottish Masters but within five years of turning pro Ebdon had reached the final of the world championships. He lost to Stephen Hendry, who registered his fifth successive title, but gained revenge with victory over the Scot in the 2002 final.

Ebdon had won the 2006 UK championship prior to competing at the Crucible so was in form as the tournament began. He recorded a 10-8 victory over Michael Holt followed by a 13-2 thrashing of David Gray before meeting Shaun Murphy in the quarter-final. The reigning champion was dispatched 13-7 but Ebdon's semi-final against Marco Fu proved to be much closer. The 26-year-old from Hong Kong pushed his opponent to the limit and was unlucky to bow out of the tournament with a 16-17 defeat as Ebdon won through to the final against Graeme Dott.

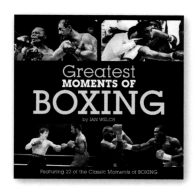

Greatest
MOMENTS OF
BOXING
by IAN WELCH

Featuring 22 of the Classic Moments of BOXING

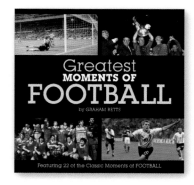

Greatest
MOMENTS OF
FOOTBALL
by GRAHAM BETTS

Featuring 22 of the Classic Moments of FOOTBALL

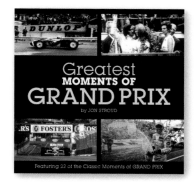

Greatest
MOMENTS OF
GRAND PRIX
by JON STROUD

Featuring 22 of the Classic Moments of GRAND PRIX

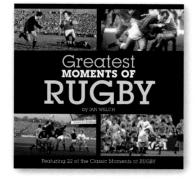

Greatest
MOMENTS OF
RUGBY
by IAN WELCH

Featuring 22 of the Classic Moments of RUGBY

THE PICTURES IN THIS BOOK WERE PROVIDED COURTESY OF THE FOLLOWING:

GETTY IMAGES
101 Bayham Street, London NW1 0AG

PA PHOTOS
www.paphotos.com

Concept and Creative Direction:
VANESSA and KEVIN GARDNER

Design and Artwork: KEVIN GARDNER

Image research: ELLIE CHARLESTON

PUBLISHED BY GREEN UMBRELLA PUBLISHING

Publishers:
JULES GAMMOND and VANESSA GARDNER

Written by: IAN WELCH